I Can't See

Written by Suzanne Hardin • Illustrated by Marc Mongeau

Celebration Press
An Imprint of Addison-Wesley
Educational Publishers, Inc.

I can't see the movie.

I can't see the road.

I can't see the pizza.

I can't see the numbers.

I can't see the mail.

I can't see the teacher . . .

but I CAN see the parade!